C000299098

Prayers of The Last Prophet

Prayers of The Last Prophet

By
YUSUF ISLAM

MOUNTAIN *of* LIGHT

© 1998 Yusuf Islam

This edition first published in 1998
Reprinted with minor corrections in 2000

Published by Mountain of Light
Mountain of Light Productions Ltd PO Box 7404 London N7 8JQ UK
Mountain of Light South Africa (PTY) LTD PO Box 43486 Industria 2042 South Africa
Astrolabe Islamic Media 201 Davis Dr Suite I Sterling VA 20164 USA

www.mountainoflight.com

British Library Cataloguing in Publication Data
A catalogue record of this book is available
from The British Library

Printed in Italy

ISBN 1900675 05 6 Hardback
ISBN 1900675 20 X CD
ISBN 1900675 21 8 Cassette

C O N T E N T S

Introduction

Introduction

IN A WORLD of phenomenal, unrelenting change and, sadly, diminishing spirituality – where modern man has naïvely crowned himself conqueror of all and sundry – some things remain untouched and preserved from the harsh blasts of what passes for progress and modernity. The Qur'an and the canonical sayings of the Prophet Muhammad, *ṣalla Allāhu 'alayhi wa sallam*, stand firm as beacons of spiritual guidance in a world of materialism, unchanged and divinely shielded. Divine revelation and Prophetic example together serve as the believer's guide, taking him through each and every aspect of his life, showing him the right way that brings forth Allah Most High's bountiful mercy and good pleasure.

This book, as its title suggests, focuses on one particular aspect: prayer, in Arabic *du'ā*. It contains a small selection of prophetic supplications and Qur'anic verses, and is the accompanying book to the CD and cassette of the same name. *Prayers Of The Last Prophet* ﷺ has been produced with all humility in an effort to present just a few of the many supplications proffered by our beloved Prophet, *ṣalla Allāhu 'alayhi wa sallam*. It in no way replaces (nor seeks to) the many splendid works from past and present scholars that elucidate upon and illuminate the prayers of Allah Most High's last Messenger.

Supplication is man's monologue to God. It is the act of calling out, whether it be for assistance or guidance. It is something innate within mankind, believer and non-believer alike, and may take a profane or spiritual guise. Everyone of us will seek and call out, particularly in times of need. Yet all too often, once the need is alleviated through divine mercy, the suppliant forgets. As Allah Most High says in the Qur'an:

> When distress seizes you at sea those that ye call upon besides Himself leave you in the lurch! But when He brings you back safe to land ye turn away (from Him). Most ungrateful is man! [1]

In contrast, the true believer will supplicate not only in times of distress but predominantly when times are good. He is aware of his limitations, penitent, humble, grateful and God conscious (*taqwā*). His *du'ās* are a fundamental part of his worship and permeate every facet of his life.

As you glance through the pages, you will notice that the *du'ās* presented here deal with matters mundane as well as matters significant; from supplicating before one eats or travels to prayers seeking Allah Most High's guidance and the Garden of Eternity. Each prayer, regardless of subject, is imbued with weighty words and yet weightier meaning, and because they are largely non-obligatory, their supererogatory nature increases their spiritual efficacy.

Unlike *ṣalāt* or ritual prayer, which is bound by conditions of time, place, orientation and movement, the believer may supplicate to his Lord and Master as he so chooses, utilising the language and words within which he finds best expression. There is, however, greater *baraka* or blessing in memorising and reciting in Arabic the *du'ās* used by our beloved Prophet, *ṣalla Allāhu 'alayhi wa sallam* – the most perfect example of man – who would supplicate long and hard and taught his followers to do the same. Imitating prophetic expression, *prima facie* formulaic, presents the believer with an excellent opportunity to gain his Creator's pleasure. Such *du'ās*, recited constantly and earnestly, are sure to bring the believer closer to Allah Most High. They are the believers' *aide-mémoire*. These prayers remind man of his true nature and calling as God's vicegerent upon this earth for a time preordained. Moreover, they highlight the ephemeralness of this world, and give significant perspective to what may otherwise seem senseless and chaotic. Remembering their Lord, beseeching His help and guidance and seeking His protection from the weaknesses of one's *nafs* or self desires, as well as from the whisperings of the accursed Satan, form the foundation of each supplication.

The ritual prayer apart, *du'ā* is the only other time when Man formally communicates with God. It is a direct channel to one's Creator and is provided as a mercy and blessing to mankind. Allah Most High says:

> Supplicate to Me and I will answer you [2]

For He is mindful of His Creation; He is *Ghafūrun Raḥeem*. Though Allah Most High encourages supplication, He is in no way in need of it or for that matter anything else. Nor does His creation affect or diminish Him in any way. His mercy and bounty is without limit.

> And if all the trees in the earth were pens, and the sea, with seven more seas to help it, (were ink), the words of Allah could not be exhausted. Allah is Mighty, Wise. [3]

When the believer is in earnest supplication to his Lord he draws himself closer to Him. Though he may be engrossed in a personal and private appeal to Allah borne of circumstance, seeking assistance or respite, he is brought nearer. The very act of supplication is an act of remembrance of Allah, a meritorious act that has the ability to bestow solace upon the believer [4]. In making *du'ā*, man affirms his dependence upon God, he places his trust in Him and he praises Him. Allah Most High in return hears his supplication and answers it.

We trust this selection of prayers will serve as a gentle introduction to one of the most profound and beautiful aspects of man's worship. We hope it may inspire you to make these *du'ās* part of your life and encourage others to do the same.

All praise is due to Allah Most High, Lord of the Worlds and may He send His choicest salutations and peace upon the Seal of the Prophets, Muhammad, and upon his Family and Companions together, *Aameen*.

TAYYEB SHAH 1419H / 1998 CE

REFERENCES:
1.   17:67
2.   60:40
3.   31:27
4.   In the Remembrance of Allah do hearts find satisfaction (13:28)

ACKNOWLEDGEMENTS:
Zafar Ashraf, Rashid Ayyub, Iman Omran, Dr Muhammad Isa Waley,
Ayman Abdul Haleem, Khaleel Muhammad

PHOTOCREDITS:
Peter Sanders, Stockbyte Photos, Ali Kazuyoshi Namachi and Alistair Duncan

DESIGN:
Abd-al Lateef Whiteman and Yusuf Islam

PROJECT MANAGER:
Tayyeb Shah

The Prayers

أَعُوذُ بِاللهِ مِنَ الشَّيْطَانِ الرَّجِيمِ

بِسْمِ اللهِ الرَّحْمَنِ الرَّحِيمِ

وَإِذَا سَأَلَكَ عِبَادِى عَنِّى فَإِنِّى قَرِيبٌ
أُجِيبُ دَعْوَةَ الدَّاعِ إِذَا دَعَانِ
فَلْيَسْتَجِيبُوا لِى وَلْيُؤْمِنُوا بِى لَعَلَّهُمْ يَرْشُدُونَ ◆

When my servants ask thee concerning Me, I am indeed
close (to them): I listen to the prayer of every suppliant
when he calls on Me: Let them also with a will listen to
My call, and believe in Me: that they may walk in
the right way.[1]

∾

O SON OF ADAM On the authority of Anas, may Allah be pleased with him, who said, "I heard the Messenger of Allah, *ṣalla Allāhu ʿalayhi wa sallam* (may the blessings and peace of Allah be upon him), say, 'Allah the Almighty has said:

O son of Adam, so long as you call upon Me and ask of Me, I shall forgive you for what you have done and I shall not mind. O son of Adam, were your sins to reach the clouds of the sky and were you then to ask forgiveness of Me, I would forgive you. O son of Adam, were you to come to Me with sins nearly as great as the earth and were you then to face Me, ascribing no partner to Me, I would bring you forgiveness as close to it in measure.'" [2]

اَللّٰهُمَّ إِنِّىْ أَسْأَلُكَ فَوَاتِحَ الْخَيْرِ وَ خَوَاتِمَهُ وَ جَوَامِعَهُ وَ أَوَّلَهُ وَ آخِرَهُ وَ ظَاهِرَهُ وَبَاطِنَهُ وَ الدَّرَجَاتِ الْعُلىٰ مِنَ الْجَنَّةِ آمِيْنَ.

Oh Allah! I beg of You all the openings of goodness and its endings and its completeness and perfection, its first and last, its outwardness and inwardness, and the highest places in Paradise. *Aameen.* [3]

∾

THE FĀTIHAH

بِسْمِ اللَّهِ الرَّحْمَنِ الرَّحِيمِ

الْحَمْدُ لِلَّهِ رَبِّ الْعَالَمِينَ ◇

الرَّحْمَنِ الرَّحِيمِ ◇ مَلِكِ يَوْمِ الدِّينِ ◇

إِيَّاكَ نَعْبُدُ وَإِيَّاكَ نَسْتَعِينُ ◇ اهْدِنَا

الصِّرَاطَ الْمُسْتَقِيمَ ◇ صِرَاطَ الَّذِينَ أَنْعَمْتَ

عَلَيْهِمْ غَيْرِ الْمَغْضُوبِ عَلَيْهِمْ

وَلَا الضَّالِّينَ ◆ آمِينَ

In the name of Allah, the Merciful, the Most Kind. Praise be to
Allah. Lord of the Worlds, the Merciful, the Most Kind: Owner
of the Day of Judgement, You (alone) do we worship, You
(alone) do we ask for help. Show us the straight path, the path of
those You have favoured; not the path of those who earn Your
anger, nor of those who go astray. *Aameen.* [4]

On the authority of Abu Hurayrah, may Allah be pleased with him, the Prophet, ṣalla Allāhu 'alayhi wa sallam, said, "When the Imam says *Aameen* then you should all say *Aameen*, for the angels say *Aameen* at that time and he whose *Aameen* coincides with the *Aameen* of the angels all his past sins will be forgiven." [5]

اَللَّهُمَّ إِنِّىْ أَسْأَلُكَ خَيْرَ الْمَسْأَلَةِ وَ خَيْرَ الدُّعَاءِ وَ خَيْرَ النَّجَاحِ وَ خَيْرَ الْعَمَلِ
وَخَيْرَ الثَّوَابِ وَ خَيْرَ الْحَيَاةِ وَ خَيْرَ الْمَمَاتِ.

O Allah, I beg of You the best of requests, the best of the prayers, the best of success, the best of the deeds, the best of the rewards, the best of life and the best of death. [6]

∾

On the authority of Abu 'Abbas 'Abdullah the son of 'Abbas, may Allah be pleased with them both, who said, "One day I was behind the Prophet, ṣalla Allāhu 'alayhi wa sallam, and he said to me, 'Young man, I shall teach you some words of advice. 'Be mindful of Allah and Allah will protect you. Be mindful of Allah and you will find Him in front of you. If you ask, ask of Allah. If you seek help, seek help of Allah. Know that if the nation were to gather together to benefit you with anything it would benefit you only with something that Allah had already prescribed for you and that if they gathered together to harm you with anything they would harm you only with something Allah had already prescribed for you. The pens have been lifted and the pages have dried.'"[7] And Abu Hurayrah reported that the Messenger of Allah, ṣalla Allāhu 'alayhi wa sallam, said, "When someone of you prays, let him not say, 'O Allah forgive me if that is Your wish.' But let him be firm in conviction and cherish a great hope and Allah does not consider anything too great which He is able to grant." [8]

BE MINDFUL OF ALLAH

∾

5

≈

RABBĪ YĀ
RAHMĀN

My Lord, O Merciful One!
My Lord, O Merciful One!
My Lord, O Merciful One!
My Lord, O Merciful One!
My Lord, O Merciful One!
My Lord, O Merciful One!

رَبِّيْ يَا رَحْمٰنْ   رَبِّيْ يَا رَحْمٰنْ
رَبِّيْ يَا رَحْمٰنْ   رَبِّيْ يَا رَحْمٰنْ
رَبِّيْ يَا رَحْمٰنْ   رَبِّيْ يَا رَحْمٰنْ

≈

My Lord, O Merciful One!
My Lord, O Merciful One!
My Lord, O Merciful One!
Grant me ease in my affairs,
My Lord, O Merciful One!
Bless me with (Your) Forgiveness,
And open up my breast!

رَبِّيْ يَا رَحْمٰنْ   رَبِّيْ يَا رَحْمٰنْ
رَبِّيْ يَا رَحْمٰنْ   يَـسِّرْلِـيْ أَمْرِيْ
وَامْنَحْنِى الْغُفْرَانْ   وَاشْرَحْ لِيْ صَدْرِيْ

≈

My Lord, O Merciful One!
My Lord, O Merciful One!
My Lord, O Merciful One!
My Lord, O Merciful One!
Grant me strong faith,
And enlighten my heart.

رَبِّيْ يَا رَحْمٰنْ   رَبِّيْ يَا رَحْمٰنْ
رَبِّيْ يَا رَحْمٰنْ   رَبِّيْ يَا رَحْمٰنْ
وَارْزُقْنِي الْإِيْمَانْ   نَوِّرْ لِيْ قَلْبِـــيْ

≈

6

≋

My Lord, O Merciful One!
My Lord, O Merciful One!
My Lord, O Merciful One!
My Lord, O Merciful One!
And make the Qur'an to me
A guidance for my intellect.

رَبِّـى ْ يَا رَحْمَـنْ   رَبِّـى ْ يَا رَحْمَـنْ
رَبِّـي ْ يَا رَحْمَـنْ   رَبِّـي ْ يَا رَحْمَـنْ
وَاجْعَلْ لِى الْقُرْآنْ   يَهْدِي لِي عَقْلِيْ

≋

My Lord, O Merciful One!
My Lord, O Merciful One!
My Lord, O Merciful One!
Grant me ease in my affairs,
My Lord, O Merciful One!
Bless me with (Your) Forgiveness,
And open up my breast!

رَبِّـي ْ يَا رَحْمَـنْ   رَبِّـي ْ يَا رَحْمَـنْ
رَبِّـي ْ يَا رَحْمَـنْ   يَـسِّرْ لِـي ْ أَمْرِيْ
وَامْنَحْنِى الْغُفْرَانْ   وَاشْرَحْ لِيْ صَدْرِيْ

≋

My Lord, O Merciful One!
My Lord, O Merciful One!
My Lord, O Merciful One!
My Lord, O Merciful One!
Forgive me for my sin
My Lord, O Merciful One![9]

رَبِّـي ْ يَا رَحْمَـنْ   رَبِّـي ْ يَا رَحْمَـنْ
رَبِّـي ْ يَا رَحْمَـنْ   رَبِّـي ْ يَا رَحْمَـنْ
اِغْفِـرْ لِي ْ ذَنْــبِيْ   رَبِّـي ْ يَا رَحْمَـنْ

≋

7

❦

On the authority of Shaddad ibn Aws, may Allah be pleased with him, the Prophet, *salla Allāhu 'alayhi wa sallam*, said, "The chief of prayers for forgiveness is:

اللَّهُمَّ أَنْتَ رَبِّي لاَ إِلَهَ إِلاَّ أَنْتَ، خَلَقْتَنِي وَ أَنَا عَبْدُكَ، وَ أَنَا عَلَى عَهْدِكَ وَ وَعْدِكَ

مَا اسْتَطَعْتُ، أَعُوذُ بِكَ مِنْ شَرِّ مَا صَنَعْتُ، أَبُوءُ لَكَ بِنِعْمَتِكَ عَلَيَّ، وَ أَبُوءُ بِذَنْبِيْ

فَاغْفِرْ لِي إِنَّهُ لاَ يَغْفِرُ الذُّنُوْبَ إِلاَّ أَنْتَ.

O Allah, you are my Lord, there is no God but You. You created me and I am Your servant and I will keep my covenant and promise to you as much as I can. I seek refuge with You from all the evil I have done. I admit before You Your blessings upon me and I admit to You all my sins. So forgive me. Certainly none can forgive sins except You." The Prophet, *salla Allāhu 'alayhi wa sallam*, added, "If somebody recites it during the day with firm faith in it and dies on the same day before the evening, he will be from the people of Paradise and if somebody recites it at night with firm faith in it and dies before the morning he will be from the people of Paradise." [10]

❦

اَللّٰهُمَّ إِنَّا نَسْأَلُكَ خَيْرَ هَذِهِ اللَّيْلَةِ فَتْحَهَا وَ نَصْرَهَا وَ نُوْرَهَا وَ بَرْكَتَهَا وَ هُدَاهَا

وَ نَعُوْذُ بِكَ مِنْ شَرِّ مَا فِيْهَا وَ شَرِّ مَا بَعْدَهَا .

O Allah, we beg of You the good of this night, the victory of it, the help
of it, the light of it, the blessing of it and the guidance of it; and we seek
refuge in You from whatever evil is within it and whatever evil
comes after it.[11]

On the authority of al-Bara' ibn 'Azib, may Allah be pleased with
him, who said, "The Messenger of Allah, *salla Allāhu 'alayhi wa
sallam*, said to me, 'When you want to go to bed, perform *wuḍū'*
(ablution) as you do for prayers, then lie down on your right side
and say:

اَللّٰهُمَّ أَسْلَمْتُ وَجْهِيْ إِلَيْكَ، وَ فَوَّضْتُ أَمْرِيْ إِلَيْكَ، وَ أَلْجَأْتُ ظَهْرِيْ إِلَيْكَ،

رَغْبَةً وَ رَهْبَةً إِلَيْكَ، لَا مَلْجَأَ وَ لَا مَنْجَى مِنْكَ إِلَّا إِلَيْكَ، آمَنْتُ بِكِتَابِكَ الَّذِيْ

أَنْزَلْتَ، وَ بِنَبِيِّكَ الَّذِيْ أَرْسَلْتَ .

O Allah, I have surrendered my face to You and I am under Your
command; and put my trust in You expecting Your reward and
fearing Your punishment. There is no escape and no shelter from
You except to You. I believe in the Book You have revealed and in
Your Prophet You have sent.

'And should you die after reciting this you will die on a natural
religion; so let these words be the last you say before going to
bed.'" [12]

تَتَجَافَىٰ جُنُوبُهُمْ عَنِ ٱلْمَضَاجِعِ يَدْعُونَ رَبَّهُمْ
خَوْفًا وَطَمَعًا وَمِمَّا رَزَقْنَـٰهُمْ يُنفِقُونَ ۝
فَلَا تَعْلَمُ نَفْسٌ مَّآ أُخْفِىَ لَهُم مِّن قُرَّةِ أَعْيُنٍ جَزَآءًۢ
بِمَا كَانُوا۟ يَعْمَلُونَ ◆

They forsake their beds of sleep to call on their Lord, in fear and
hope: and they spend (in charity) out of that which We have
bestowed on them. Now no soul knows what delights of the eye
are kept hidden (in reserve) for them — as a reward for their
(good) deeds.[13]

∾

Narrated Abu Hurayrah, may Allah be pleased with him, "The
Messenger of Allah, ṣalla Allāhu 'alayhi wa sallam, said, 'When it is
the last third of the night, Our Lord, the Blessed, the Superior,
descends to the nearest heaven each and every night and says: Is
there anyone who calls Me, that I may respond to his call? Is there
anyone who asks Me for something, that I may give it to him? Is
there anyone who asks My forgiveness, that I may forgive him?'" [14]

∾

And on the authority of Ibn 'Abbas, may Allah be pleased with him, "When the Prophet, *ṣalla Allāhu 'alayhi wa sallam*, got up at night to offer the night prayer, he used to say,

اَللَّهُمَّ لَكَ الْحَمْدُ، أَنْتَ نُوْرُ السَّمَاوَاتِ وَ الأَرْضِ وَ مَنْ فِيْهِنَّ، وَ لَكَ الْحَمْدُ،

أَنْتَ قَيِّمُ السَّمَاوَاتِ وَ الأَرْضِ وَ مَنْ فِيْهِنَّ. وَ لَكَ الْحَمْدُ، أَنْتَ الْحَقُّ وَ وَعْدُكَ

حَقٌّ، وَ قَوْلُكَ حَقٌّ، وَلِقَاؤُكَ حَقٌّ، وَالْجَنَّةُ حَقٌّ، وَ النَّارُ حَقٌّ، وَ السَّاعَةُ حَقٌّ،

وَ النَّبِيُّوْنَ حَقٌّ، وَمُحَمَّدٌ حَقٌّ، اَللَّهُمَّ لَكَ أَسْلَمْتُ، وَعَلَيْكَ تَوَكَّلْتُ وَبِكَ آمَنْتُ،

وَ إِلَيْكَ أَنَبْتُ، وَ بِكَ خَاصَمْتُ، وَ إِلَيْكَ حَاكَمْتُ، فَاغْفِرْ مَا قَدَّمْتُ وَمَا أَخَّرْتُ،

وَ مَا أَسْرَرْتُ وَ مَا أَعْلَنْتُ. أَنْتَ الْمُقَدِّمُ وَ أَنْتَ الْمُؤَخِّرُ، لاَ إِلَهَ إِلاَّ أَنْتَ.

'O Allah, all praises are for You. You are the Light of the Heavens and the Earth and whatever is in them and all praises are for You. You are the Sustainer of the heavens and the earth and whatever is in them and all praises are for You. You are the Truth and Your promise is true, and Your words are true, and the meeting with You is true, and Paradise is true, and Hell is true, and the Hour is true, and the Prophets are true and Muhammad is true (*ṣalla Allāhu 'alayhi wa sallam*). O Allah, I surrender myself to You and I depend on You, and I believe in You, and I turn in repentance to You, and on Your account I quarrel and to You I turn in judgement. So please forgive my past and my future sins, and whatever I have done in secret and whatever I have done in public. You are the Expediter and You are the Delayer; there is no God but You.'" [15]

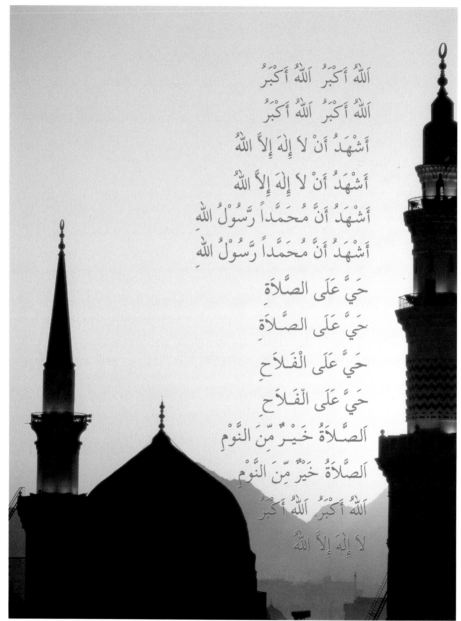

اَللهُ أَكْبَرُ اَللهُ أَكْبَرُ

اَللهُ أَكْبَرُ اَللهُ أَكْبَرُ

أَشْهَدُ أَنْ لَا إِلهَ إِلاَّ اللهُ

أَشْهَدُ أَنْ لَا إِلهَ إِلاَّ اللهُ

أَشْهَدُ أَنَّ مُحَمَّداً رَّسُوْلُ اللهِ

أَشْهَدُ أَنَّ مُحَمَّداً رَّسُوْلُ اللهِ

حَيَّ عَلَى الصَّلَاةِ

حَيَّ عَلَى الصَّلَاةِ

حَيَّ عَلَى الْفَلَاحِ

حَيَّ عَلَى الْفَلَاحِ

اَلصَّلَاةُ خَيْرٌ مِّنَ النَّوْمِ

اَلصَّلَاةُ خَيْرٌ مِّنَ النَّوْمِ

اَللهُ أَكْبَرُ اَللهُ أَكْبَرُ

لَا إِلهَ إِلاَّ اللهُ

اَللَّهُمَّ رَبَّ هَذِهِ الدَّعْوَةِ التَّامَّةِ وَالصَّلَاةِ الْقَائِمَةِ آتِ مُحَمَّداً الْوَسِيْلَةَ والْفَضِيْلَةَ وَابْعَثْهُ مَقَاماً مَحْمُوْداً الَّذِي وَعَدْتَّهُ

O Allah! Lord of this perfect call and of the *salāh* to be established. (Kindly) give Muhammad the right of intercession and also superiority; and elevate him to the praised position which Thou hast promised him. [17]

On the coming of dawn the Prophet, *ṣalla Allāhu 'alayhi wa sallam*, used to say in his prayers:

LIGHT

اَللَّهُمَّ اجْعَلْ فِيْ قَلْبِيْ نُوْراً، وَفِيْ بَصَرِيْ نُوْراً، وَ فِيْ سَمْعِيْ نُوْراً، وَ عَنْ يَمِيْنِيْ نُوْراً، وَ عَنْ يَسَارِيْ نُوْراً، وَ فَوْقِيْ نُوْراً، وَتَحْتِيْ نُوْراً، وَأَمَامِيْ نُوْراً، وَ خَلْفِيْ نُوْراً، وَاجْعَلْ لِيْ نُوْراً.

"O Allah, illuminate my heart with light, and my eyes with light and my ears with light and let there be light on my right and light on my left. Let there be light above me and light below me, let there be light in front of me and light behind me. O Allah, make me a light." [18]

Abu Malik reported that the Messenger of Allah, *ṣalla Allāhu 'alayhi wa sallam*, said, "When one of you awakens to the day let him say:

THE MORNING

أَصْبَحْنَا وَ أَصْبَحَ الْمُلْكُ لله رَبِّ الْعَالَمِيْنَ، اَللَّهُمَّ إِنِّيْ أَسْأَلُكَ خَيْرَ هَذَا الْيَوْمِ فَتْحَهُ وَ نَصْرَهُ وَ نُوْرَهُ وَ بَرَكَتَهُ وَ هُدَاهُ وَ أَعُوْذُ بِكَ مِنْ شَرِّ مَا فِيْهِ وَ شَرِّ مَا بَعْدَهُ.

We have entered the morning and the kingdom has awakened for Allah, Lord of the Worlds. O Allah, verily I beg of You the good of this day, the victory of it and the help of it, the light of it and the blessings of it and its guidance. And I seek protection in You from whatever evil is within it and whatever evil comes after it." [19]

15

إِنْ سَأَلْتُمْ عَنْ إِلَهِي فَهُوَ رَحْمَنٌ رَحِيم

أَنْزَلَ الشَّرْعَ حَنِيفاً رَحْمَةً لِلْعَالَمِين ـ رَحْمَةً لِلْعَالَمِين

إِنْ سَأَلْتُمْ عَنْ كِتَابِي فَهُوَ قُرْآنٌ كَرِيم

ضَمَّ دُسْتُورَ الْحَيَاتِ وَ حَوَى النُّورَ الْمُبِين ـ وَ حَوَى النُّورَ الْمُبِين

If you ask me who my God is, on whose Name I call,
If you ask me who my God is: 'He's the God of us all – Allah, the Merciful.'
If you ask me what my Book is that I hold in my hand,
If you ask me what my Book is: 'It's the Holy Qur'an, the Holy Qur'an.'

إِنْ سَأَلْتُمْ عَنْ نَبِيِّي فَهُوَ إِنْسَانٌ عَظِيم

عَلَّمَ النَّاسَ عُلُوماً جَمَعَ الدُّنْيَا وَ دِين ـ جَمَعَ الدُّنْيَا وَ دِين

إِنْ سَأَلْتُمْ عَنْ عَدُوِّي فَهُوَ شَيْطَانٌ رَجِيم

خَائِنٌ يَدْعُو لِكُفْرٍ وَ يُعِينُ الْمُعْتَدِينَ ـ وَ يُعِينُ الْمُعْتَدِينَ

If you ask me who my Prophet is, I will say, 'Haven't you heard?
His name is Muhammad, ṣalla Allāhu 'alayhi wa sallam,
A Mercy to the worlds, a Mercy to the worlds.'
If you ask me who my enemy is, I will say, 'Don't you know?'
If you ask me who my enemy is: 'He's that same old Devil, that same old Devil.'[20]

إِنْ سَأَلْتُمْ عَنْ إِلَهِي فَهُوَ رَحْمَنٌ رَحِيم

إِنْ سَأَلْتُمْ عَنْ كِتَابِي فَهُوَ قُرْآنٌ كَرِيم ـ فَهُوَ قُرْآنٌ كَرِيم

إِنْ سَأَلْتُمْ عَنْ نَبِيِّي فَهُوَ إِنْسَانٌ عَظِيم

إِنْ سَأَلْتُمْ عَنْ عَدُوِّي فَهُوَ شَيْطَانٌ رَجِيم أَعُوذُ بِاللهِ مِنَ الشَّيْطَانِ الرَّجِيم

رَبَّنَا ظَلَمْنَا أَنْفُسَنَا وَ إِنْ لَّمْ تَغْفِرْلَنَا وَتَرْحَمْنَالَنَكُونَنَّ مِنَ الْخَاسِرِينَ

Our Lord, we have wronged our own souls: if You
forgive us not and bestow not upon us Your mercy, we shall
certainly be lost.[21]

LET NOT
OUR HEARTS
DEVIATE

رَبَّنَا لَاتُزِغْ قُلُوبَنَا بَعْدَ إِذْ هَدَيْتَنَاوَهَبْ
لَنَامِن لَّدُنكَ رَحْمَةً إِنَّكَ أَنتَ الْوَهَّابُ ◆

Our Lord, let not our hearts deviate now after
You have guided us, but grant us mercy
from Your very presence; for You are
the Grantor of bounties without measure.[22]

17

Narrated Jabir, "The Prophet, *ṣalla Allāhu 'alayhi wa sallam*, used to teach us the *Istikhārah*, a special prayer for deciding each and every matter, as he used to teach us Surahs from the Holy Qur'an; he used to say, 'If any one of you intends to do something he should offer two *rak'ats* of prayer, other than the obligatory prayer, and then say:

اَللّٰهُمَّ إِنِّيْ أَسْتَخِيْرُكَ بِعِلْمِكَ، وَ أَسْتَقْدِرُكَ بِقُدْرَتِكَ، وَ أَسْأَلُكَ مِنْ فَضْلِكَ الْعَظِيْمِ، فَإِنَّكَ تَقْدِرُ وَ لَا أَقْدِرُ، وَ تَعْلَمُ وَ لَا أَعْلَمُ، وَ أَنْتَ عَلَّامُ الْغُيُوْبِ. اَللّٰهُمَّ إِنْ كُنْتَ تَعْلَمُ أَنَّ هَذَا الْأَمْرَ خَيْرٌ لِيْ فِيْ دِيْنِيْ وَ مَعَاشِيْ وَ عَاقِبَةِ أَمْرِيْ فَاقْدُرْهُ لِيْ. وَ إِنْ كُنْتَ تَعْلَمُ أَنَّ هَذَا الْأَمْرَ شَرٌّ لِيْ فِيْ دِيْنِيْ وَ مَعَاشِيْ وَ عَاقِبَةِ أَمْرِيْ فَاصْرِفْهُ عَنِّيْ وَ اصْرِفْنِيْ عَنْهُ وَ اقْدُرْ لِيَ الْخَيْرَ حَيْثُ كَانَ، ثُمَّ رَضِّنِيْ بِهِ.

O Allah, I seek Your preference through Your knowledge and seek from You ability through Your power and beg You for Your infinite bounty, for You have power and I have none and You have knowledge but I know not, and You are the Knower of the Unseen. O Allah, if You know that this matter is good for me in my religion, for my livelihood and for the consequences of my affairs then ordain it for me; and if You know that this matter is evil for me in my religion, for my livelihood and for the consequences of my affairs then turn it away from me and turn me away from it and choose what is good for me wherever it may be and make me pleased with it.' After saying this, then he should mention and name his difficulty and his need." [23]

اَللّٰهُمَّ آتِنَا فِي الدُّنْيَا حَسَنَةً وَ فِي الْآخِرَةِ حَسَنَةً وَقِنَا عَذَابَ النَّارِ.

On the authority of Anas, may Allah be pleased with him, "The most frequent prayer of the Prophet, *ṣalla Allāhu 'alayhi wa sallam*, was, 'O Allah, grant to us goodness in this world and goodness in the Hereafter and save us from the punishment of the fire.'" [24]

قُلِ ٱللَّهُمَّ مَٰلِكَ ٱلْمُلْكِ تُؤْتِى ٱلْمُلْكَ مَن تَشَآءُ وَتَنزِعُ ٱلْمُلْكَ

مِمَّن تَشَآءُ وَتُعِزُّ مَن تَشَآءُ وَتُذِلُّ مَن تَشَآءُ بِيَدِكَ ٱلْخَيْرُ

إِنَّكَ عَلَىٰ كُلِّ شَىْءٍ قَدِيرٌ ◇ تُولِجُ ٱلَّيْلَ فِى ٱلنَّهَارِ وَتُولِجُ ٱلنَّهَارَ

فِى ٱلَّيْلِ وَتُخْرِجُ ٱلْحَىَّ مِنَ ٱلْمَيِّتِ وَتُخْرِجُ ٱلْمَيِّتَ مِنَ ٱلْحَىِّ

وَتَرْزُقُ مَن تَشَآءُ بِغَيْرِ حِسَابٍ ◈

Say: O Allah, Owner of Sovereignty, You give sovereignty to
whom You will, and You take sovereignty from whom You will:
You exalt whom You will, and You bring low whom You will:
in Your hand is all Good. Truly You have Power over all things.
You cause the night to pass into the day, and You cause the day
to pass into the night. You bring the living out of the dead, and
You bring the dead out of the living; and You give sustenance to
whom You will, without measure.[25]

When leaving the home a person should always remember to put his trust in Allah and say:

$$\text{بِسْمِ اللهِ، تَوَكَّلْتُ عَلَى اللهِ وَ لَاحَوْلَ وَ لَا قُوَّةَ إِلَّا بِاللهِ.}$$

"In the name of Allah, I place my trust in Allah and there is no might nor power except with Allah." [26]

When mounting a horse or boarding any vehicle at the start of a journey the Prophet, *salla Allāhu 'alayhi wa sallam*, taught us to say:

$$\text{اَللهُ أَكْبَرُ، اَللهُ أَكْبَرُ، اَللهُ أَكْبَرُ سُبْحَانَ الَّذِيْ سَخَّرَ لَنَا هَذَا وَ مَاكُنَّا لَهُ مُقْرِنِيْنَ}$$

$$\text{وَ إِنَّا إِلَىٰ رَبِّنَا لَمُنْقَلِبُوْنَ.}$$

"Allah is the Greatest! Allah is the Greatest! Allah is the Greatest! How perfect is He, the One who has placed His transport at our service and we alone would not have been capable of that; and to our Lord is the final return."

And if the journey was a fair distance then he used to say:

$$\text{اَللَّهُمَّ إِنَّا نَسْأَلُكَ فِيْ سَفَرِنَا هَذَا الْبِرَّ وَ التَّقْوَى، وَ مِنَ الْعَمَلِ مَاتَرْضَى، اَللهُمَّ}$$

$$\text{هَوِّنْ عَلَيْنَا سَفَرَنَا هَذَا واطْوِ عَنَّا بُعْدَهُ، اَللَّهُمَّ أَنْتَ الصَّاحِبُ فِى السَّفَرِ،}$$

$$\text{وَ الْخَلِيْفَةُ فِي الأَهْلِ، اَللهُمَّ إِنِّي أَعُوْذُ بِكَ مِنْ وَعْثَاءِ السَّفَرِ، وَ كَآبَةِ الْمَنْظَرِ}$$

$$\text{وَ سُوْءِ الْمُنْقَلَبِ فِى الْمَالِ وَ الأَهْلِ.}$$

"O Allah, we ask of You the righteousness and piety of this journey of ours and we ask You for deeds which please You. O Allah, make our journey easy and let us cover its distance quickly. O Allah, You are the Companion on the journey and the Successor over the family. O Allah, I take refuge with You from the difficulties of travel, from beholding a miserable sight and from an ill-fated return in my wealth and family." [27]

اَللَّهُمَّ بَارِكْ لَنَا فِيْهَا، اَللَّهُمَّ ارْزُقْنَا جَنَاهَا وَ حَبِّبْنَا إِلَى أَهْلِهَا وَ حَبِّبْ صَالِحِي أَهْلِهَآ إِلَيْنَا.

O Allah, bless us in this (township). O Allah, provide us with the fruits thereof and make us beloved to its people and make its pious people beloved to us.[28]

◈

VISITING
THE SICK

وَإِذَا مَرِضْتُ فَهُوَ يَشْفِينِ ◇ وَالَّذِى يُمِيتُنِى ثُمَّ يُحِيِينِ ◇ وَالَّذِى أَطْمَعُ أَن يَغْفِرَلِى خَطِيئَتِى يَوْمَ الدِّينِ رَبِّ هَبْ لِى حُكْمًا وَأَلْحِقْنِى بِالصَّالِحِينَ ◆

And when I sicken then He heals me; He causes me to die then gives me life (again): and I sincerely hope He will forgive my sin on the Day of Judgement. My Lord, grant me wisdom and unite me with the righteous.[29]

❧

'Ali ibn Abu Talib, may Allah be pleased with him, related that he heard the Messenger of Allah, ṣalla Allāhu 'alayhi wa sallam, say, "If a man calls on his sick Muslim brother it is as if he walks reaping the fruits of Paradise until he sits; and when he sits, he is showered in mercy; and if this was in the morning, seventy thousand angels send prayers upon him until the evening, and if this was in the evening, seventy thousand angels send prayers upon him until the morning." SEVENTY THOUSAND ANGELS

And when the Prophet, ṣalla Allāhu 'alayhi wa sallam, would enter upon a sick person he would say:

$$لَا بَأْسَ طَهُورٌ إِنْ شَاءَ اللّٰهُ.$$

"No harm! May this be a purification for you, if Allah wills."[30]

Also, it is said that any Muslim servant who visits a sick person whose prescribed moment of death has not arrived and then prays the following seven times:

$$أَسْأَلُ اللّٰهَ الْعَظِيْمَ رَبَّ الْعَرْشِ الْعَظِيْمِ أَنْ يَشْفِيَكَ.$$

"I ask Allah the Supreme, Lord of the Magnificent Throne to cure you." And if his prescribed moment of death has not arrived then he, the sick person, will be cured.[31]

❧

And when the time for prayer came, the Prophet, ṣalla Allāhu 'alayhi wa sallam, would make his way to the Mosque. He would step in with his right foot and then say:

أَعُوْذُ بِاللهِ الْعَظِيْمِ وَ بِوَجْهِهِ الْكَرِيْمِ وَ سُلْطَانِه الْقَدِيْمِ مِنَ الشَّيْطَانِ الرَّجِيْمِ، بِسْمِ اللهِ، وَالصَّلَاةُ وَالسَّلَاْمُ عَلَى رَسُوْلِ اللهِ، اَللَّهُمَّ افْتَحْ لِيْ أَبْوَابَ رَحْمَتِكَ.

"I take refuge with Allah, the Supreme, and by His Noble Face and His Eternal Authority, from the accursed Devil; in the name of Allah, and blessings and peace be upon the Messenger of Allah. O Allah, open the gates of Your Mercy for me."[32]

قُلْ إِنَّ صَلَاتِي وَنُسُكِي وَمَحْيَايَ وَمَمَاتِي لِلَّهِ رَبِّ الْعَالَمِينَ ◇ لَا شَرِيكَ لَهُ وَبِذَٰلِكَ أُمِرْتُ وَأَنَا أَوَّلُ الْمُسْلِمِينَ ◆

Truly, my prayer, my sacrifice, my living and my dying are for Allah, Lord of the Worlds, no partner has He: this I have been commanded, and I am the first of the Muslims.[33]

WATER, ICE
AND SNOW
After the Prophet, ṣalla Allāhu 'alayhi wa sallam, had entered the prayer he would make the following supplication:

اَللَّهُمَّ بَاعِدْ بَيْنِيْ وَ بَيْنَ خَطَايَايَ كَمَا بَاعَدْتَ بَيْنَ الْمَشْرِقِ وَ الْمَغْرِبِ، اَللَّهُمَّ نَقِّنِيْ مِنْ خَطَايَايَ كَـمَـايُنَقَّى الثَّـوْبُ الأَبْيَضُ مِنَ الدَّنَسِ، اَللَّهُمَّ اغْـسِلْنِي مِنْ خَطَايَايَ بِالْمَاءِ وَ الثَّلْجِ وَالْبَرَدِ.

"O Allah, separate me far from my sins as You have separated the East and West. O Allah, cleanse me of my sins as white cloth is cleansed from dirt. O Allah, wash me of my sins with water, ice and snow."[34]

❧

PROSTRATION
The Prophet, ṣalla Allāhu 'alayhi wa sallam, said, "The slave is closest to his Lord when he is prostrating, so increase supplication in it."[35]

اَللَّهُمَّ إِنِّيْ أَسْأَلُكَ الْجَنَّةَ وَ مَا قَرَّبَ إِلَيْهَا مِنْ قَوْلٍ أَوْ عَمَلٍ وَ أَعُوْذُ بِكَ مِنَ النَّارِ وَ مَا قَرَّبَ إِلَيْهَا مِنْ قَوْلٍ أَوْ عَمَلٍ وَ أَسْأَلُكَ أَنْ تَجْعَلَ كُلَّ قَضَاءٍ لِيْ خَيْرًا وَ أَسْأَلُكَ مَا قَضَيْتَ لِيْ مِنْ أَمْرٍ أَنْ تَجْعَلَ عَاقِبَتَهُ رُشْدًا.

"O Allah, I seek of You Paradise and that word and deed which draws me near to it; and I seek refuge in You from the Fire and that word and deed which draws me near to it. I beg of You that You should make every decree good for me and I beg of You that whatever You have decreed, You make its end come right."[36]

❧

اَلتَّحِيَّاتُ لله، وَ الصَّلَوَاتُ وَ الطَّيِّبَاتُ، اَلسَّلاَمُ عَلَيْكَ أَيُّهَا النَّبِيُّ

وَ رَحْمَةُ اللهِ وَ بَرَكَاتُهُ ، اَلسَّلاَمُ عَلَيْنَا وَ عَلَى عِبَادِ اللهِ الصَّالِحِينَ،

أَشْهَدُ أَنْ لاَ إِلهَ إِلاَّ اللهُ وَحْدَهُ لاشَرِيكَ لَهُ وَ أَشْهَدُ أَنَّ مُحَمَّداً عَبْدُهُ وَ رَسُولُهُ.

اَللَّهُمَّ صَلِّ عَلَى مُحَمَّدٍ وَعَلَى آلِ مُحَمَّدٍ كَمَا صَلَّيْتَ عَلَى إِبْرَاهِيمَ

وَعَلَى آلِ إِبْرَاهِيمَ إِنَّكَ حَمِيدٌ مَجِيدٌ، اَللَّهُمَّ بَارِكْ عَلَى مُحَمَّدٍ

وَعَلَى آلِ مُحَمَّدٍ كَمَا بَارَكْتَ عَلَى إِبْرَاهِيمَ وَعَلَى آلِ إِبْرَاهِيمَ

إِنَّكَ حَمِيدٌ مَجِيدٌ.

All greetings, prayers and good words are due to Allah. Peace be on you,
O Prophet and also the Mercy of Allah and His blessings. Peace be upon
us and upon the righteous slaves of Allah. I bear witness that there is no
God but Allah alone and He has no partner, and I bear witness that
Muhammad is His slave and Messenger. O Allah, send prayers on
Muhammad, and on the family of Muhammad, as You sent prayers on
Ibrahim and on the family of Ibrahim; You are indeed Worthy of Praise,
Full of Glory. O Allah, send blessings on Muhammad and on the family
of Muhammad, as You sent blessings on Ibrahim and the family of
Ibrahim; You are indeed Worthy of Praise. Full of Glory. [37]

～

اَللَّهُمَّ أَعِنِّيْ عَلَى ذِكْرِكَ، وَ شُكْرِكَ، وَ حُسْنِ عِبَادَتِكَ.

"O Allah, help me to remember You, to thank You and to worship You in the best of manners."[38]

اَللَّهُمَّ إِنِّيْ أَعُوْذُ بِكَ مِنْ عَذَابِ الْقَبْرِ، وَ أَعُوْذُ بِكَ مِنْ فِتْنَةِ الْمَسِيحِ الدَّجَّالِ، وَ

أَعُوْذُ بِكَ مِنْ فِتْنَةِ الْمَحْيَا وَ الْمَمَاتِ، اَللَّهُمَّ إِنِّيْ أَعُوْذُ بِكَ مِنَ الْمَأْثَمِ وَ الْمَغْرَمِ.

"O Allah, truly I seek refuge with You from the punishment of the grave and I seek refuge with You from the trials of the false Christ and I seek refuge with You from the trials of living and dying. O Allah, truly I seek refuge with You from sin and debt."[39]

And when the Prophet, *ṣalla Allāhu 'alayhi wa sallam*, had finished the prayer he used to step out of the Mosque with his left foot first and say:

اَللَّهُمَّ إِنِّيْ أَسْأَلُكَ مِنْ فَضْلِكَ.

"O Allah, I beg of You Your Bounty."[40]

～

بِسْمِ ٱللَّهِ ٱلرَّحْمَٰنِ ٱلرَّحِيمِ

أَلْهَىٰكُمُ ٱلتَّكَاثُرُ ◇ حَتَّىٰ زُرْتُمُ ٱلْمَقَابِرَ ◇ كَلَّا سَوْفَ
تَعْلَمُونَ ◇ ثُمَّ كَلَّا سَوْفَ تَعْلَمُونَ ◇ كَلَّا لَوْ تَعْلَمُونَ
عِلْمَ ٱلْيَقِينِ ◇ لَتَرَوُنَّ ٱلْجَحِيمَ ◇ ثُمَّ لَتَرَوُنَّهَا
عَيْنَ ٱلْيَقِينِ ◇ ثُمَّ لَتُسْأَلُنَّ يَوْمَئِذٍ عَنِ ٱلنَّعِيمِ ◆

The rivalry in worldly increase diverts you (from the more
serious things), until you visit the graves. But, yea, you soon
shall know (the reality). Again, you soon shall know! Yea,
were you to know now with certainty of mind, (you would
beware!) You should certainly see Hellfire! Again, you shall
see it with certainty of sight! Then, shall ye be questioned
that Day about the pleasures (ye indulged in).[41]

31

Ibn Mas'ud reported that the Messenger of Allah, *ṣalla Allāhu 'alayhi*
wa sallam, said, "I prohibited you from visiting graves but visit them now because they teach renunciation of the world and remind of the Hereafter." [42]

And when the Prophet, *ṣalla Allāhu 'alayhi wa sallam*, was asked what to say when visiting the graves, he said, "Say:

اَلسَّـلاَمُ عَلَيْكُمْ أَهْلَ الدِّيَارِ مِنَ الْمـؤْمِنِيْنَ وَ الْمُـسْلِمِـيْنَ وَ إِنَّا إِنْ شَـاءَ اللهُ بِكُمْ لاَحِقُوْنَ نَسْأَلُ اللّٰهَ لَنَا وَ لَكُمُ الْعَافِيَةَ.

Peace be upon you all, O inhabitants of the graves, amongst the believers and the Muslims. Verily we will, if Allah wishes, be united with you. We ask Allah for well-being for us and for you." [43]

اَللّٰهُمَّ اغْفِرْ لِحَيِّنَا وَ مَيِّتِنَا وَ شَاهِدِنَا، وَ غَائِبِنَا وَ صَغِيْرِنَا وَ كَبِيْرِنَا، وَ ذَكَرِنَا وَ أُنْثَانَا. اَللّٰهُمَّ مَنْ أَحْيَيْتَهُ مِنَّا فَأَحْيِه عَلَى الْإِسْلاَمِ وَ مَنْ تَوَفَّيْتَهُ مِنَّا فَتَوَفَّهُ عَلَى الْإِيْمَانِ.

O Allah, forgive our living and our dead, those present and those absent, our young and our old, our males and our females.
O Allah, whomever of us You keep alive, then let such a life be upon Islam, and whom amongst us You take unto Yourself, then let such a death be upon faith. [44]

ENTERING
THE HOME

When the Prophet, *ṣalla Allāhu 'alayhi wa sallam*, arrived home, as he entered he would say:

بِسْمِ اللهِ وَلَجْنَا، وبِسْمِ اللهِ خَرَجْنَا، وَ عَلَى رَبِّنَا تَوَكَّلْنَا.

"In the name of Allah we enter and in the name of Allah we leave, and upon our Lord we place our trust." [45]

GRANT US
WIVES &
OFFSPRING

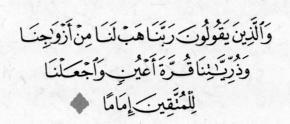

And those who pray, 'Our Lord, grant us wives and offspring who will be the comfort of our eyes; and give us (the grace) to lead the righteous.' [46]

◞

PRAYER FOR
CHILDREN

The Messenger of Allah, *ṣalla Allāhu 'alayhi wa sallam*, used to always show affection and kindness to children. He used to kiss them and say a prayer for them, asking Allah to place them under His protection:

$$ أُعِيْذُكُمْ بِكَلِمَاتِ اللهِ التَّامَّةِ مِنْ كُلِّ شَيْطَانٍ وَ هَامَّةٍ وَ مِنْ كُلِّ عَيْنٍ لامَّةٍ. $$

"I commend you to the protection of Allah's perfect words from every devil, venomous creature, and every evil eye."[47]

PRAYER FOR
PARENTS

And to the elderly, the Prophet, *ṣalla Allāhu 'alayhi wa sallam*, would always attend and show mercy. He prayed for them as Allah Almighty inspired him with the words:

$$ وَاخْفِضْ لَهُمَا جَنَاحَ الذُّلِّ مِنَ الرَّحْمَةِ وَقُل رَّبِّ ارْحَمْهُمَا كَمَا رَبَّيَانِى صَغِيْراً. $$

"And out of kindness lower to them the wing of humility and say, 'My Lord bestow on them Thy mercy even as they cared for me when I was little.'"[48]

◞

إِنْ سَأَلْتُمْ

إِنْ سَأَلْتُمْ عَنْ إِلَهِيْ فَهُوَ رَحْمَنٌ رَحِيْم

أَنْزَلَ الشَّرْعَ حَنِيْفاً رَحْمَةً لِلْعَالَمِيْن

If you ask me who my God is, on whose name I call,
If you ask me who my God is: 'He's the God of us all – Allah, the
Merciful.'

إِنْ سَأَلْتُمْ عَنْ كِتَابِيْ فَهُوَ قُرْآنٌ كَرِيْم

ضَمَّ دُسْتُورَ حَيَاتِيْ وَ حَوَى النُّوْرَ الْمُبِيْن

If you ask me what my Book is that I hold in my hand,
If you ask me what my Book is: 'It's the Holy Qur'an, the Holy
Qur'an.'

إِنْ سَأَلْتُمْ عَنْ نَبِيِّيْ فَهُوَ إِنْسَانٌ عَظِيْم

عَلَّمَ النَّاسَ عُلُوْماً جَمَعَ الدُّنْيَا وَ دِين

If you ask me who my Prophet is, I will say, 'Haven't you heard?
His name is Muhammad, ṣalla Allāhu 'alayhi wa sallam,
A Mercy to the worlds, a Mercy to the worlds.'

إِنْ سَأَلْتُمْ عَنْ عَدُوِّي فَهُوَ شَيْطَانٌ رَجِيْم

خَائِنٌ يَدْعُو لِكُفْرٍ وَ يُعِيْنُ الْمُعْتَدِيْنَ ـ وَ يُعِيْنُ الْمُعْتَدِيْن

If you ask me who my enemy is, I will say, 'Don't you know?'
If you ask me who my enemy is: 'He's that same old Devil, that
same old Devil.'[49]

≈

37

〜

When the Prophet, *ṣalla Allāhu 'alayhi wa sallam*, sat down to eat, he would always mention the name of Allah. And on the authority of Jābir [may Allah be pleased with him], the Prophet, *ṣalla Allāhu 'alayhi wa sallam*, said, "When a man enters his house and then remembers Allah at the time of entering and before taking his food, the Devil says to himself, 'No shelter for you this night and no supper.' And when he enters it and does not remember Allah at the time of entering it the Devil says to himself, 'You have taken shelter for the night.' And when he does not remember Allah at the time of taking food the Devil says, 'You have taken shelter for the night and supper too.'" [50]

And after finishing a meal the Prophet, *ṣalla Allāhu 'alayhi wa sallam*, would say:

$$\text{اَلْحَمْدُ لِلّٰهِ الَّذِي أَطْعَمَنَا وَ سَقَانَا وَ جَعَلَنَا مِنَ الْمُسْلِمِيْنَ.}$$

"Praise be to Allah who fed us and gave us drink and made us Muslims." [51]

〜

On the authority of Abu Dharr al-Ghifari, may Allah be pleased
with him, who said that, "Among the sayings the Prophet, *salla
Allāhu 'alayhi wa sallam*, relates from His Lord, may He be glorified,
is that He said, 'O My servants, I have forbidden oppression for
Myself and have made it forbidden amongst you, so do not
oppress one another. O My servants, all of you are astray except for
those I have guided; so seek guidance of Me and I shall guide you.
O My servants, all of you are hungry except for those I have fed; so
seek food of Me and I shall feed you. O My servants, all of you are
naked except for those I have clothed; so seek clothing of Me and I
shall clothe you. O My servants, you sin by night and by day and I
forgive all sins; so seek forgiveness of Me and I shall forgive you. O
My servants, you will not attain harming Me so as to harm Me and
you will not attain benefiting Me so as to benefit Me. O My
servants, were the first of you and the last of you, the human of you
and the jinn of you, to be as pious as the most pious heart of any one
man of you, that would not increase My Kingdom in anything. O
My servants, were the first of you and the last of you, the human of
you and the jinn of you, to be as wicked as the most wicked heart of
any one man of you, that would not decrease My Kingdom in
anything. O My servants, were the first of you and the last of you,
the human of you and the jinn of you, to rise up in one place and
make a request of Me and were I to give everyone what he
requested, that would not decrease what I have any more than a
needle decreases the sea if put into it [then taken out with water on
it]. O My servants, it is but your deeds that I reckon up for you and
then recompense you for; so let him who finds good praise Allah
and let him who finds other than that blame no one but himself.'" [52]

إِنَّ ٱللَّهَ وَمَلَٰٓئِكَتَهُۥ يُصَلُّونَ عَلَى ٱلنَّبِيِّ يَٰٓأَيُّهَا ٱلَّذِينَ ءَامَنُوا۟ صَلُّوا۟ عَلَيْهِ وَسَلِّمُوا۟ تَسْلِيمًا ◆

Allah and His angels send blessings on the Prophet.
O you who believe! Send your blessings on him and salute him
with a worthy salutation.[13]

اَللّٰهُمَّ إِنِّى أَسْأَلُكَ يَا اَللّٰهُ يَا رَحْمٰنُ يَارَحِيمُ يَاجَارَ الْمُسْتَجِيرِيْنَ يَاأَمَانَ

الْخَائِفِينَ يَاعِمَادَ مَنْ لَاۤ عِمَادَ لَهُ يَاسَنَدَ مَنْ لَا سَنَدَ لَهُ يَاذُخْرَ مَنْ لَا

ذُخْرَ لَهُ يَا حِرْزَ الضُّعَفَاءِ يَاكَنْزَ الْفُقَرَاءِ يَاعَظِيمَ الرَّجَاءِ يَامُنْقِذَ

الْهَلْكٰى يَامُنْجِىَ الْغَرْقٰى يَامُحْسِنُ يَامُنْعِمُ يَاجَبَّارُ يَا مُنِيرُ يَا أَنْتَ الَّذِى

سَجَدَ لَكَ سَوَادُ اللَّيْلِ وَضَوْءُ النَّهَارِ وَشُعَاعُ الشَّمْسِ وَنُورُ الْقَمَرِ

وَخَفِيقُ الشَّجَرِ وَدَوِىُّ الْمَاءِ يَا اَللّٰهُ أَنْتَ اللّٰهُ لَا إِلٰهَ لَا أَنْتَ إِلاَّ أَنْتَ لَا شَرِيْكَ لَكَ

أَسْئَلُكَ أَنْ تُصَلِّىَ عَلٰى سَيِّدِنَا مُحَمَّدٍ ﴿ صَلَّى اللّٰهُ عَلَيْهِ وَسَلَّمَ ﴾

عَبْدِكَ وَرَسُوْلِكَ وَعَلٰى آلِ سَيِّدِنَا مُحَمَّدٍ ﴿ صَلَّى اللّٰهُ عَلَيْهِ وَسَلَّمَ ﴾

O Allah, I beg of Thee, O God, O Merciful, O Compassionate;
O Protector of the Seeker of Protection; O Protection of the
horror-stricken; O Pillar of one who has no pillar, and O
Supporter of one who has no support; O Provisioner of one who
has no provision; O the Guardian of the weak; O Treasurer of
the poor; O Great One on whom one can place hopes;
O Deliverer of the ruined and Rescuer of the drowning;
O Good One, O Benefactor, O Compellor, O Illuminating! Thou
art One before Whom the darkness of night, the brightness of
the day, the ray of the sun, and the light of the moon, the
rustling of the trees, and the reverberation of waters showed
submission. O Allah, Thou art Allah! There is no partner with
You, I beg of You that You shower blessings on Muhammad
(ṣalla Allāhu 'alayhi wa sallam), Your servant and Your
Messenger, and on the family of Muhammad
(ṣalla Allāhu 'alayhi wa sallam).[54]

ṢALLI ʿALĀ
MUHAMMAD

اَللّٰهُمَّ صَلِّ عَلٰى مُحَمَّدٍ اَللّٰهُمَّ صَلِّ عَلٰى مُحَمَّدٍ

اَللّٰهُمَّ صَلِّ عَلٰى مُحَمَّدٍ اَللّٰهُمَّ صَلِّ عَلٰى مُحَمَّدٍ

O Allah, send Your peace on Your slave, Muhammad
O Allah, send Your blessings on Your beloved,
O Allah, send Your peace on Your slave, Muhammad
Grant Your ceaseless mercy, Lord, to Your blessed Prophet,

اَللّٰهُمَّ صَلِّ عَلٰى مُحَمَّدٍ اَللّٰهُمَّ صَلِّ عَلٰى مُحَمَّدٍ

O Allah, send Your peace on the people of his house
As You sent Your peace upon *Nabī* Ibrahim and his house
O Allah, send Your peace upon the people of his house
And all those who follow him, till the coming of the hour

اَللّٰهُمَّ صَلِّ عَلٰى مُحَمَّدٍ اَللّٰهُمَّ صَلِّ عَلٰى مُحَمَّدٍ

اَللّٰهُمَّ صَلِّ عَلٰى مُحَمَّدٍ

O Allah! Raise him up to that praised lofty place
Grant him that approach to Thee and to Thy Grace
O Allah! Raise him up to that praised lofty place
On the Day his enemies, they will be disgraced.[55]

اَللّٰهُمَّ صَلِّ عَلٰى مُحَمَّدٍ اَللّٰهُمَّ صَلِّ عَلٰى مُحَمَّدٍ

اَللّٰهُمَّ صَلِّ عَلٰى مُحَمَّدٍ

Notes

1. Surah al-Baqarah (2): 186.
2. At-Tirmidhee.
3. Hizb al-A'zam, p. 55.
4. Surah al-Fatihah (1): 1-7.
5. Sahih al-Bukhari volume 8, p. 274.
6. Hizb al-A'zam, p. 55.
7. At-Tirmidhee.
8. Sahih al-Bukhari, volume 8, p. 235.
9. Rabbi Ya Rahman: words traditional; melody by Samira Habashi.
10. Sahih al-Bukhari, volume 8, p. 212-3.
11. Prayers of the Prophet, pp. 19-20.
12. Sahih al-Bukhari, volume 8, pp. 216-7.
13. Surah al-Sajdah (32): 16-17.
14. Sahih al-Bukhari, volume 8, p. 225.
15. Sahih al-Bukhari, volume 8, p. 221-2.
16. Translation: Allah is most Great! Allah is most Great! Allah is most Great! Allah is most Great! I bear witness that there is no god but Allah. I bear witness that there is no god but Allah. I bear witness that Muhammad is the messenger of Allah. I bear witness that Muhammad is the messenger of Allah. Come to prayer. Come to prayer. Come to success. Come to success. Prayer is better than sleep. Prayer is better than sleep. Allah is most Great! Allah is most Great! There is no god but Allah.
17. Prayers of the Prophet, p. 29.
18. Sahih al-Bukhari, volume 8, p. 221-2.
19. Abu Dawud.
20. Traditional, English words by Yusuf Islam.
21. Surah al-A'raf (7):23.
22. Surah Al 'Imran (3): 8.
23. Sahih al-Bukhari, volume 8, p. 259.
24. Sahih al-Bukhari, volume 8, p. 265.
25. Surah Al 'Imran (3): 26-27.
26. Abu Dawud & at-Tirmidhee.

27. Sahih Muslim.
28. Prayers of the Prophet, p. 45-46.
29. Surah al-Shu'ara' (26): 80-83.
30. Sahih al-Bukhari.
31. Abu Dawud & al-Tirmidhi.
32. Abu Dawud.
33. Surah al-An'am (6): 162-163.
34. Abu Dawud & Hakim.
35. Sahih Muslim.
36. Hizb al-A'zam pp. 53-54.
37. Sahih al-Bukhari, Sahih Muslim & Abu Dawud.
38. Abu Dawud & al-Nasa'i.
39. Sahih al-Bukhari & Sahih-Muslim
40. Prayers of the Prophet, p. 30.
41. Surah at-Takathur (102): 1-8.
42. Ibn Majah.
43. Sahih Muslim.
44. Ibn Majah.
45. Abu Dawud.
46. Surah al-Furqan (25): 74.
47. Sahih al-Bukhari.
48. Surah al-Isra' (17): 24.
49. See note 20.
50. Sahih Muslim.
51. Abu Dawud & at-Tirmidhee.
52. Sahih Muslim.
53. Surah al-Ahzab (33): 56.
54. Hizb al-A'zam pp. 102-103.
55. Words and melody by Yusuf Islam.

The Holy Qur'an. Text, translation and commentary by 'Abdullah Yusuf 'Ali. New Revised Edition. Brentwood, Maryland, 1409/1989.

The Holy Qur'an. English translation of the meaning and commentary of 'Abdullah Yusuf 'Ali. Revised Edition. Madinah, 1410/1990.

The Glorious Qur'an. Text and explanatory translation by Muhammad Marmaduke Pickthall, Karachi, 1977.

Sahih al-Bukhari. The translations of the meanings of Sahih al-Bukhari by Muhammad Muhsin Khan. 4th ed. Beirut, 1405/1985.

Mishkat al-Masabih: Al-Hadis. Compiled by al-Khatib al-Tabrizi. An English translation and commentary by Fazlin Karim. Lahore, n.d.

An-Nawawi's Forty Hadith. Translated by Ezzedin Ibrahim and Denys Johnson Davies. 2nd ed. Damascus, 1977.

Hizb al-A'zam. Translated by Maulana Abdul-Hamid Siddiqi. Lahore, 1975.

Prayers of the Prophet. Translated by Maulana Abdul-Hamid Siddiqi. Lahore, 1980.

The Prophet's Prayer, *sallallaahu 'alaihi wasallam.* By Shaikh Muhammad Naasir-ud-Deen al-Albaanee. Malaysia, 1413/1993

Fortification of the Muslim through remembrance and supplication from the Qur'an and Sunnah. By Sa'eed Ibn 'Ali Ibn Wahf Al-Qahtaani. Riyadh, n.d.

A is for ALLAH

DOUBLE CASSETTE   **DOUBLE CD**

It took 20 years for Yusuf Islam to develop *A is for Allah* from a song to a monumental and attractive work. The book comprises of 68 beautiful full colour pages and over 40 photographs describing, for children and adults, the essence of Islam through the Arabic alphabet. The album on Double CD and Double Cassette complements the Book and includes:

* Complete book narrated by Yusuf Islam
* Qur'anic recitation by renowned Egyptian *Qari* Sheikh Muhammad Gibreel
* English translation read by Imam Hamza Yusuf from the USA
* 8 songs - 7 arranged & written by Yusuf Islam including the title track *A is for Allah* - and introducing Zain Bhikha from South Africa
* Guest appearance by Malaysia's world famous nasheed group Raihan performing harmonies on Yusuf's *Seal of The Prophets*
* Adhan by the Muazzin of Makkah
* Approx. running time 101 minutes

Hardback Book · Double CD · Double Cassette
Cover Poster · A is for Allah Song Lyrics Poster
2 CD + Book & postcard pack
2 Cassette + Book & postcard pack

30th JUZ *of the* Holy Qur'an

Arabic recitation by Sheikh Muhammad Al-Minyaoui
English narrated by Yusuf Islam

With Islam today having over one billion followers, the Qur'an is probably the most widely read book in the world, with sections of it being recited at least five times a day by Muslims during their daily prayers.

This recording features the original Arabic recited by the respected Egyptian *Qari* Sheikh Muhammad Al-Minyaoui with each verse being followed by its English translation read by Yusuf Islam. The Arabic recitation style is *tartil* and the English narration is based upon *The Noble Qur'an* translated by Dr. Muhammad Taqi-ud-Din Al-Hilali and Dr. Muhammad Muhsin Khan.

Approx. running time 120 minutes

Double Cassette · Double CD

The Life of the Last Prophet

With over 350,000 copies sold, this spoken-word recording of the life of Prophet Muhammad ﷺ was the first official release by Yusuf Islam since his departure from the music business as Cat Stevens back in 1978. The biography is fully authenticated and approved by an international group of *'ulema* (scholars) and contains selected verses of the Qur'an, recited by the respected Egyptian *Qari* (reciter) Sheikh Muhammad Al-Minyaoui. It also includes the song *Tala'a al-Badru 'Alayna*, and a beautiful rendition of the *adhan* (call to prayer) and is the best concise biography on the Prophet Muhammad ﷺ available in English.

Approx. running time: 60 minutes

CD · Cassette · Hardback Book
Giftcase - Hardback Book + CD · Giftcase - Hardback Book + Cassette

Prayers of the Last Prophet

Prayers of The Last Prophet ﷺ is the follow-up to the hugely successful *The Life of the Last Prophet* ﷺ, and contains a collection of *du'as* (supplications) as used by the Prophet Muhammad ﷺ. Narrated by Yusuf Islam and structured around phases of the day, these *du'as* cover a range of everyday activities seeking God's guidance. All are derived from Qur'an and Hadith and are fully authenticated. *Prayers* also contains Qur'anic recitation by the acclaimed Egyptian *Qari* (reciter) the late Sheikh Mahmoud Khalil Alhousari and features 3 new songs including Yusuf Islam's *If You Ask Me*.

Approx. running time: 60 minutes

CD · Cassette · Hardback Book
Giftcase - Hardback Book + CD · Giftcase - Hardback Book + Cassette

WELCOME TO THE QUR'AN
Gateway to Faith

This is the first in the Islamic Circle Talks series, adapted from talks given by Yusuf Islam at Regent's Park Mosque, London. Here, Yusuf takes the listener on a journey of discovery as he introduces the majestic beauty of the Qur'an through the gateway of faith. Includes Qur'anic recitation by Egyptian *Qari* Ahmed Ali Abd al-Tawab and nasheed *Qur'anu Rabbee*.

Approx. running time: 48 minutes
Cassette

The Prophetic Art of
COMMUNICATION *Introduction to Da'wah*

Tape 2 in the Islamic Circle Talk series is about how the Prophets delivered God's message. This talk reminds us all of the importance of inviting people to Islam and particularly the methodology to use following the *sunnah* (example) of the last Prophet Muhammad ﷺ

Approx. running time: 39 minutes
Cassette

MOUNTAIN *of* LIGHT

www.mountainoflight.com